WRITE YOUR OWN...

CHILLERS

PIE CORBETT

**ILLUSTRATED BY
PETER BAILEY**

Belitha Press

First published in Great Britain in 2001 by

🌀 Belitha Press Limited, London House
Great Eastern Wharf
Parkgate Road, London SW11 4NQ

Series editor: Mary-Jane Wilkins
Editors: Vic Parker, Russell Mclean
Designer: Sarah Goodwin
Illustrator: Peter Bailey

ISBN 1 84138 253 1

British Library Cataloguing in Publication Data for
this book is available from the British Library.

Printed by Omnia Books Ltd, Glasgow

10 9 8 7 6 5 4 3 2 1

CONTENTS

FEEL THE CHILL

THINKING ABOUT CHILLERS

The attic door creaked open. Something rustled in the darkness. I stared, but could see nothing beyond the vague shapes of old suitcases and boxes piled high. It smelt damp. Thick dust powdered every surface.

I carefully made my way forwards, balancing on the floor beams. I kept thinking I could put my foot through the plaster and fall straight through into the room below. A cobweb brushed my face and I felt the sudden tickle of a spider crawl across my cheek.

I stopped at a pile of old camping equipment. It was a jumble of guy ropes, torn canvas, poles and wooden pegs. Then I saw the hand, quite still and white. At first I thought it was marble. But then it moved.

Exciting stuff, isn't it? It makes you want to read on. Who is exploring the attic? What are they looking for?

Most importantly, whose hand is it? If you like reading spine-chilling stories, then how about writing one too? This book will help you write your own chilling adventure.

WHAT IS A CHILLER?

Many people like nothing more than imagining a dark night in a graveyard with something frightening floating about! Any story like this that makes the air turn cold is a chiller. Chillers are truly frightening tales!

A chiller can be:
☆ a story about ghosts and hauntings;
☆ a tale about monsters;
☆ a weird, unsolved mystery;
☆ a story about a strange, supernatural event.

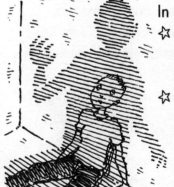

In the story there might be:
☆ ghosts, ghouls, mutants, mummies, weirdos, monsters, vampires;
☆ a heroine, a hero, loyal friends, an old woman rumoured to be a witch, a brave teacher or professor, a strange tramp, a wise museum curator, the police, an evil inventor;
☆ a run-down block of flats, a science laboratory, an enchanted wood, a ghost town, an old church, a ruined castle, a cave full of bones, a library of strange old books, a deserted road.

WHAT DO I NEED TO WRITE MY OWN CHILLER?

You don't need much equipment. I started out as a writer using just a notebook and a pen. Now I work with a computer as well. A good dictionary (or computer spell check) can be helpful. A thesaurus is also useful for looking up alternatives to words you use a lot.

Try to find a quiet place to write. I have written in all sorts of places – on trains, the tops of buses and in classrooms. Best of all, I like a place where I know my thoughts will not be disturbed.

WRITING TIP
Some of the writing terms in this book are explained in the glossary on page 62. There are checklists to help with spelling, punctuation and making new paragraphs on pages 57–59.

READ... READ... AND READ SOME MORE

The secret of being a good writer is to read a lot. Have a book on the go every day. When you read, think about:
☆ how the best stories are structured;
☆ which incidents sound exciting;
☆ how the writer keeps the pace going;
☆ how the paragraphs and sentences are written.

All writers start by imitating their favourite authors. Here are some of my favourite spine-chilling books and authors.

☆ Series

Creatures; After Dark; The Ghost Hunters (Hippo)
Goosebumps; Point Horror; Mutant Point Horror; Point Horror Unleashed (Scholastic)
Tremors (Hodder Wayland)
Dark Paths (Macmillan)
Graffix (A&C Black)
Danger Zone (Watts)
The Spook Files (Madcap)

☆ Authors

Joan Aiken
Theresa Breslin
Morris Glietzman
Robin Jarvis
Paul Jennings
Pete Johnson
Margaret Mahy
Anthony Masters
Susan Price
Celia Rees
Robert Swindells

TRAPPING IDEAS

Writers are like magpies because they steal story ideas from all over the place.

☆ Listen to what people say

You might overhear something that gives you a good idea. For instance, I recently overheard a man say: "...and then it disappeared into my skin..."

☆ Watch people

Last week I saw someone who might make a character for a chiller: an old man with a nose like a beak and cold eyes, in a long black coat...

☆ Look for the unusual

Here are two odd things I saw that sparked ideas.
1 A photograph of a dead relative who looked like me.
2 A rose flowering by a house that had burned to the ground.

☆ Be curious

Wonder about things that happen. For instance, I saw a lady taking a black cat for a walk. When she walked past a shop, the owner rushed inside. Was the shop owner afraid of the black cat?

8

☆ Look out for places that seem scary

Look for places that might be haunted or where strange things might happen. Think of alternatives to obvious settings such as a deserted house or graveyard. What about a haunted supermarket, for instance?

KEEP A WRITING JOURNAL

All the writers I know keep a writing journal – a notebook in which they jot down all their ideas so they don't forget them. Make your own now out of a jotter or exercise book – a blank notebook with a hard cover is ideal.

TIME TO WRITE

1 Start off your writing journal with a list of your favourite authors and chillers. Jot down why you like these authors and books.

2 Now start collecting some ideas. Jot down:
★ a few possible names for characters;
★ two or three places that have atmosphere;
★ strange or frightening things that have happened to you and your friends;
★ odd people and things you have seen;
★ interesting sayings that people use.

3 Use your writing journal to jot down anything you might be able to use. Always be on the lookout for good ideas.

WRITERS AT WORK

STARTING YOUR OWN STORY

All writers have five 'servants' to help them when they sit down to write: who? where? when? what? and how?

1 Who?

You need one strong 'good' character, perhaps two (such as a couple of friends). You also need one strong 'evil' character, maybe a ghost or a monster. Don't have too many main characters or it will be difficult to make them all seem real.

You can write your story as though you are the main character: *I turned to face the painting and heard the sound of heavy breathing.* Or you can write as if the action is happening to someone else: *She turned to face the painting and heard the sound of heavy breathing.*

2 Where?

The next big decision is where to set your story. If you use scary places you know well, you can add details that make the settings feel real. Don't forget that frightening things can happen in ordinary places too. For instance, your main character might be asleep, safe and sound in her bedroom, when a hand slithers out from under the bed! Another way to chill your readers is to show the same setting at different points in time. Perhaps your main character is at school one day and has a flashback – a vision of something that happened long ago – in that very classroom...

3 When?

Most stories are written in the past tense. This makes it sound as if the action has already happened: *I took a deep breath and opened the door.*

Writing in the present tense can be exciting as it sounds as if the action is happening now: *I take a deep breath and open the door.* Whatever you decide, make sure you don't slip accidentally from one tense to the other.

4 What?

You need to think up a simple idea for what happens in your story. This is called a plot outline. For instance, an inventor accidentally creates a potion that changes people into savage rats. The potion is spilled into the water system!

5 How?

You also need a trigger – an event that sets the story in motion. For example, the main character has just had an operation and is not allowed to drink water overnight. When she wakes up, people have started turning into huge rats...

Let's think a bit more about some of these five servants.

GET UNDER THE CHARACTER'S SKIN

Who will be the focus of the story – your main character? Don't forget that your readers must like your main 'good' character, or they will not read on to find out what happens. You will also need a main 'chilling' character.

Before writing, think about:

1 The characters' names

For example: Angie Atherton, Sam Carter, Red Williams.

2 Special details

Choose just a couple of details for each main character.

For example:
- ☆ Something they wear. For instance, if you put a character in a T-shirt with 'Get lost!' written on it, it suggests that this person is a loner who doesn't want friends.
- ☆ Something about how your character looks, such as an old man who has a front tooth missing.
- ☆ How your characters walk, such as a girl who is always jogging along.
- ☆ An expression they use, such as, *"Get outta here."*

3 Character type

Now decide what sort of person each character is: aggressive, happy-go-lucky, friendly, keen to lead, spiteful, unkind, brainy, bold, a misery guts, angry, etc. You could create a character with a flaw – a person who is basically nice but who is jealous or steals things, perhaps.

When you are writing, keep thinking about your character types and what that sort of person would say or do next.

WRITING TIP

Why not try writing different stories about the same character or characters?

SET THE SCENE

Choose the settings in your story to create different atmospheres. To turn your readers' blood to ice, begin your story in a familiar, ordinary setting, such as a car. Then introduce something scary, perhaps a strange tapping on the car roof. Or move your characters into a contrasting, frightening setting – you could send them for a walk down a dark lane or into a circle of standing stones.

Describing the weather, time of day and time of year can also make your story more chilling. For instance, a foggy Halloween is more chilling than a sunny spring morning.

WRITING TIP
To help create realistic settings, base them on places that you know.

PLAN THE PLOT

At the heart of your story is a good plot. Sometimes, ideas will just pop into your head. Other times, you might borrow bits of ideas from comics, films and books. Here are some ideas for scenarios.

☆ A machine comes alive and is evil...
☆ A nursery rhyme, nightmare or computer game becomes real...
☆ A local ghost story starts to come true...
☆ You discover that you have an evil twin...
☆ You wake up one morning and find that you're transforming into a creature, bit by bit...
☆ You go camping and your friends start disappearing one by one...
☆ Someone takes your photo and when it's developed, there's a stranger in the picture with you...

Before you start writing, decide on an ending. You can always change your mind if you have a better idea later. If you start with no idea of where your story is going, you may lose direction and end up rambling on without getting anywhere. It can sometimes help to write the last line before you even write the first!

PULL THE TRIGGER

Every story needs a trigger – an event that happens
in the first few paragraphs and sets the tale going.
Tease your readers to make them read on.

☆ An odd sound
The main character is
woken by humming,
howling or sobbing.

☆ A strange sight
The main character is
shopping when she sees
something weird, such as
a hound with flaming eyes,
or a distorted face.

☆ A mystery
The story starts with someone telling the main character
a secret or giving them a strange warning.

☆ A wish
The main character makes a foolish wish, such as for
everlasting life, or great beauty or wealth.

☆ A lie
The tale begins with a lie. For example, a man says that
a weird animal will not bite, or that a potion is harmless.

SHAPING UP

The simplest story pattern starts with everything being all right. Then events happen which build the story. A complication produces a problem or dilemma. The rest of the story is about solving this. This pattern is like walking up and down a hill.

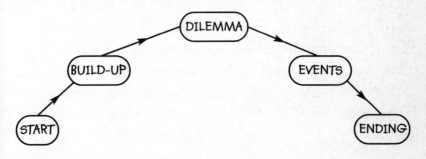

Other stories begin with the dilemma, to grip the reader from the start. Then the reader is filled in on what has already happened. The rest of the story solves the dilemma. This pattern is like walking down hill.

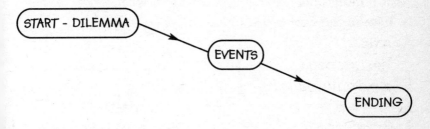

Chillers often have exciting cliffhangers – points in the story where your main character is left in deadly danger. The shape of this type of plot can be like a series of hills (see next page).

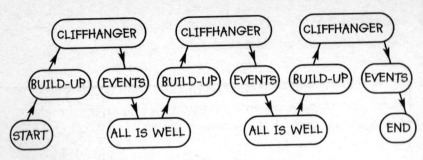

To organize your plot, decide which shape you would like to use and write it out in your writing journal. Underneath each part of the shape, jot down what will happen in your story. You could start with the basic plot shape, like this:

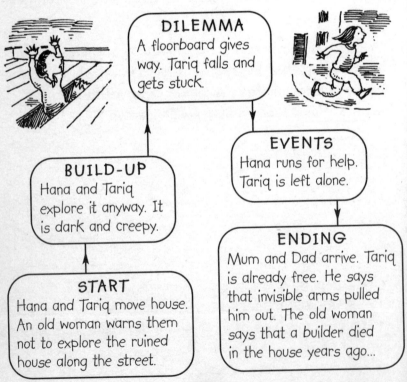

DILEMMA
A floorboard gives way. Tariq falls and gets stuck.

EVENTS
Hana runs for help. Tariq is left alone.

BUILD-UP
Hana and Tariq explore it anyway. It is dark and creepy.

ENDING
Mum and Dad arrive. Tariq is already free. He says that invisible arms pulled him out. The old woman says that a builder died in the house years ago...

START
Hana and Tariq move house. An old woman warns them not to explore the ruined house along the street.

You might then decide to change your plot
to a different shape, like this:

START – DILEMMA

Hana and Tariq are exploring an old house
when he falls through the floorboards and
gets stuck. Hana runs for help.

EVENTS

Tariq thinks about how he wouldn't be
in this mess if they hadn't just moved
to this area, and if they had listened to
the old woman who warned them not to
go exploring. Suddenly, Tariq feels cold,
invisible hands pulling him free!

ENDING

Hana and Mum and Dad arrive. They
don't believe Tariq. Later, the old woman
tells them that a builder died years ago
during the construction of the building...

Or you might want to try the third
different plot shape, perhaps like this:

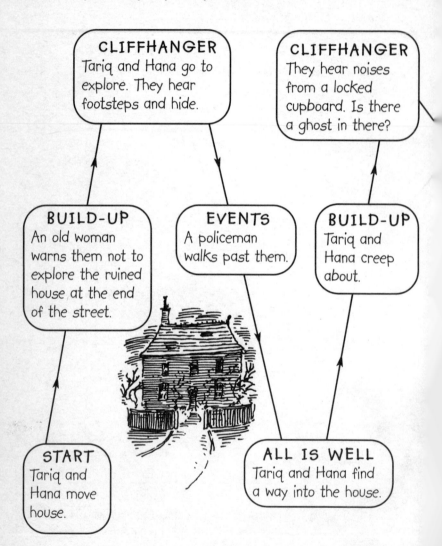

CLIFFHANGER
Tariq and Hana go to
explore. They hear
footsteps and hide.

CLIFFHANGER
They hear noises
from a locked
cupboard. Is there
a ghost in there?

BUILD-UP
An old woman
warns them not to
explore the ruined
house at the end
of the street.

EVENTS
A policeman
walks past them.

BUILD-UP
Tariq and
Hana creep
about.

START
Tariq and
Hana move
house.

ALL IS WELL
Tariq and Hana find
a way into the house.

CLIFFHANGER
Tariq falls through the attic floor and gets stuck.

EVENTS
They find the key and open it.

BUILD-UP
Tariq and Hana climb to the attic.

EVENTS
Hana runs for help. Ghostly arms lift Tariq free.

ALL IS WELL
All they find is a nest of mice.

ENDING
Mum and Dad do not believe Tariq. The old woman tells them that a builder died in the house years ago.

You could make your plot either simpler or more detailed, as you like. Remember that some parts of your plot could end up as more than one paragraph of writing. Also, as you write your story, you may find other ideas creeping in.

Your story planner will give you a start and a direction for your story, but be prepared to change direction if you have good ideas as you write.

TIME TO WRITE

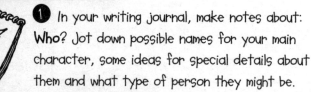

1 In your writing journal, make notes about:

Who? Jot down possible names for your main character, some ideas for special details about them and what type of person they might be.

Where? Write down some ideas for settings.

When? Make notes about what time of day your story might start. What is the weather like? Will you write your story in the present or the past?

What? Jot down some basic plot outlines to choose from.

How? Write ideas for triggers to get your story going.

2 Draw a story planner and decide on the shape you want your story to take.

TRICKS OF THE TRADE

HOW TO HYPNOTISE YOUR READERS

All the best writers do a lot of thinking before they start to write their stories. Once you have your characters, setting and plot outline, you need to think about the words and sentences you will use to tell your story. This chapter lets you in on a few tricks of the trade that writers use to make their stories really chilling.

MAKE YOUR CHARACTERS SEEM REAL

1 Describing your characters

To make your characters seem real, you need to describe their appearance. Don't give too much detail. For instance, if you describe a character as having cold eyes, you may not need to say more. Your readers will have met unfriendly people before and will have their own picture of the character.

You could think about:

☆ **How they talk**

For example, *a sharp, harsh voice* suggests an unpleasant person; *a rich laugh* suggests a kind person.

☆ **How they walk**

For example, *He strode into the room* suggests someone in charge.

☆ **What their features are like**

For example, if you give a character *a red, bulbous nose* it suggests that they drink too much; an eccentric, brainy teacher might have *a wild mop of jet black hair*.

☆ **What their clothes are like**

For example: *Jo stared at Sam's red jeans. Who on earth did he think he was?*

2 Describing what your characters do

When you are writing, keep thinking about what your characters might do in certain situations. Think about your character's type. Ask yourself: How would this character feel now? What would they do?

Imagine you have a main character, called Susie, who is offered a plate of buns. What does she do?

☆ If Susie is polite – *Susie selected the smallest bun and rested it on her plate between nibbles.*

☆ If Susie is greedy – *Susie grabbed a bun and scoffed it.*

☆ If Susie is nervous – *Susie chewed the bun and tried to swallow, but it stuck hard in her throat.*

☆ If Susie is suspicious – *Susie eyed the buns warily and left them untouched.*

WRITING TIP

You can describe your main character through what your other characters say, do or think.

For example: "Siri always puts his foot in it," mumbled Jenna.

Or: Jenna pulled back from Siri, staring at his miserable face.

Or: Jenna wondered to herself whether Siri would ever be happy.

3 Making your characters talk

Try to make your characters sound real. Some people use long, complicated words; other people like slang; some people use a favourite expression all the time. Throughout your story, think carefully about your character's type and how your character feels. This will help you decide what they would say.

Use adverbs to tell your readers how a character speaks. A character might speak slowly or carefully, quietly, loudly, cautiously, savagely, angrily, cruelly, fearlessly, bravely, firmly and so on. You might also want to use a speech verb now and then. For example: he muttered or mumbled, whispered, moaned, groaned, hissed, spat, snarled, growled, bellowed, roared, snapped.

Beware! Too much speech can be confusing. Limit your characters' conversations to three or four exchanges at a time.

☆ Don't use adverbs or speech verbs all the time, or they lose their power. For example:

> "Hi there, Tom," shouted Jo.
> "Good to see you," replied Tom.
> "Let's go to the park," stated Jo.
> "OK, if you pay my bus fare," answered Tom.

26

☆ If you use 'said' all the time with an adverb, your dialogue will sound peculiar:

> "Hi there, Tom," Jo said quietly.
> "Good to see you," Tom said calmly.
> "Let's go to the park," Jo said enthusiastically.
> "OK, if you pay my bus fare," Tom said gratefully.

WRITING TIP

Use dialogue to move your plot forwards, for example: "Let's go down to the dump," said Carl.
To help your reader picture what is happening as a character speaks, add a supporting action. For instance: "It started as a dream," groaned Tony, as he picked up the clown's mask.

PREMONITIONS

You could start your chiller with the main character having a premonition – a strong sense that something unpleasant is going to happen. This could be:

☆ **A feeling**

For example: *Suddenly Ka felt cold to her very bones. She knew she had to get out of the woods fast!*

☆ A warning

For example, the main character has a dream in which she foresees something dreadful: *Ka woke, sweating, fighting her way out of the nightmare. She had had it three nights running. A hand came towards her. A hand that turned into a claw. A claw which grabbed her face...*

Other warnings could be a fortune-teller's prediction, or breaking a mirror (which some people believe means seven years of bad luck), or something sinister that keeps appearing, such as an ugly doll or a big black raven. You could have a CD that plays a creepy message, a mobile phone that talks, or a mysterious e-mail.

WRITING TIP
Remember that to make your readers scared, describe familiar places and everyday events, and then introduce an unusual note.

GHOSTS, GHOULS, MUTANTS AND MONSTERS

To build up maximum tension, keep your ghost, ghoul, mutant or monster hidden for as long as possible. Just give your readers hints, clues and little glimpses, and let their imagination run riot. You can give them:

☆ **Sounds**

A hiss, grunt, groan, moan, scream, breathing, scratching, scraping, slithering...

☆ **Sights**

A shadow moving, red eyes glinting, a withered hand, a tongue flickering, a claw, green slime, sharp teeth...

☆ **Smells**

Rotten eggs, bad blood, acrid stale breath, decaying flesh, a sickly sweet stench...

☆ **Textures**

Rough, scaly, jagged, damp, chill, burning, oozing...

☆ **Flavours**

Bitter, sharp, stale, acid, medicine-like, fizzing...

When you reveal your ghost, ghoul, mutant or monster at last, just give one or two carefully chosen details, such as the mouth, the eyes, the teeth or the hands. Then describe how your monster moves or the sounds it makes. Your readers will picture the rest from stories they've read, films they've seen and nightmares they've had.

Add to the chilling effect by revealing your monster through the eyes of your main character, for instance: *It moved with surprising swiftness for something so big. Ka stared as it raised its arm – she saw the sharp claws and the sudden flash of blood-red eyes. This is it, she thought...*

WORD-WATCHING

Words can give you great power. If you choose your words well, you'll be able to make your reader laugh, cry, or shiver with fright. But if you choose badly, your characters will seem dull, your settings vague and your action lame.

Let's see what we can do with the words in a sentence: *The woman got out of the car.* That's pretty dull, isn't it? There are a number of ways we could improve it:

☆ Change the nouns so they are more precise: *Mrs Granby got out of the Skoda.*

☆ Change the verb so it is more powerful: *The woman clambered out of the car.*

☆ Add adjectives: *The tall woman got out of the sleek car.*

☆ Add adverbs: *The woman got slowly out of the car.*
☆ Add to the beginning of the sentence: *Although she had miles to go, the woman got out of her car.*
☆ Add to the end of the sentence: *The woman got out of the car because she could smell burning.*

☆ Rearrange the sentence: *Out of the car got the woman.*
☆ Trim the sentence: *The woman got out.*

Beware of using too many adjectives; they can make your writing sound wordy. For instance: *The tall, slim, elegant woman got out of the new, shiny, bright, sleek car.*

It's the same with adverbs. Often, you can get rid of an adverb altogether if you think of a stronger verb. For instance, you could write: *The woman got awkwardly out of the car* as: *The woman struggled out of the car.*

STUNNING SPECIAL EFFECTS

All writers have a few techniques to create different effects in their writing. Try using these special effects to make your writing more powerful.

1 Similes

A simile is a descriptive way of comparing one thing to another. Try using them to describe ghosts, ghouls, mutants and monsters. Either use the word 'like': *Its tongue flickered like a snake's.* Or use the word 'as': *Its eyes were as small as beads.*

2 Metaphors

A metaphor is a bit like a simile. In a simile, you say that one thing is *like* another. In a metaphor, you say that one thing *is* another. For example, this is a simile: *The moon was like a silver claw, reaching down to the dark pine trees.* This is a metaphor: *The silver claw of the moon reached down to the dark pine trees.*

3 Personification

You use personification when you give human qualities to an animal or object. For example: *The wind whispered. The trees gossiped. The curtains clutched at me.* Personification makes objects seem alive. This can be very frightening.

4 Alliteration

Alliteration is the repetition of similar sounds, close together. This can make a line atmospheric. In this example, the sound 's' is repeated: *The stark stars stared at me.*

5 Onomatopoeia

When you write a word that sounds like its meaning, you are using onomatopoeia. For example: *As the skeleton rose slowly from the floor, its bones cricked and cracked.*

6 Tension builders

When I was small, I was woken in the middle of the night by a scratching noise from behind the curtain. I lay awake paralysed with fear. The sound continued – a frantic scrabbling. In the end I forced myself to look. It was only my hamster, escaped from its cage! Incidents like this can build tension in a chiller. Think about all the times you've felt threatened and afraid, and the threat has turned out to be nothing at all. Here are some other ideas.

☆ Hearing voices

You are alone, but suddenly hear voices in another room. Is it ghostly intruders? No – it's only a radio!

☆ Humming machines

Late at night, you hear a strange humming coming from the kitchen. Is it an alien? No – it's the fridge!

33

☆ Following footsteps

You hear footsteps behind you that stop when you stop and speed up when you speed up. You race home – to find that the sole of your shoe has been flapping loose, making a sound like footsteps following you. You have scared yourself!

☆ Tapping

You hear a soft tapping at your window... It turns out to be the wind blowing a tree branch against the glass.

☆ Ghostly touch

You are alone. Something brushes against your leg... it's the cat!

☆ Nightly visitors

You are woken by something tickling your face. It feels like the nails of a clutching, grasping, ghostly hand... but it is only a mouse running over your bed!

☆ Treading on things

You are exploring a dark, deserted house. You tread on something that squishes under your foot. Is is monster slime? Is it the flesh of devoured creatures? No – you have trodden on a slug!

JUST FOR STARTERS

He went down the road. He went into the shop. He bought a loaf of bread. He came outside. He crossed the road. A car nearly hit him. He was frightened.

If all your sentences begin the same way, your writing will be boring. Here are some ways to vary the start of your sentences and keep your readers' attention.

☆ Start with an adverb:
  Silently, he crept towards the door.

☆ Start with a word that ends in 'ing': *Shivering, she waited.*

☆ Start with a word that ends in 'ed': *Terrified, he stared into the flaming eyes.*

☆ Start with a prepositional phrase. *Beside the atomic generator lay a puddle of thick green slime.*

WRITING TIP

Try to avoid starting sentences with 'and' or 'but' – particularly at the start of a new paragraph. Some writers do this occasionally to create a particular effect. For example, you might end a chapter with: But they were too late. Or you could end a story with: And so they made their way home. In most cases, beginning a sentence with 'and' or 'but' is thought to be bad grammar.

STYLISH SENTENCES

What do you think of this paragraph?
*Bryan walked out of the school gates.
He gazed across the town. It was
raining. The streets were deserted.
The old factory loomed in front of
him. He stared at it. No one worked
there any more. Its doors were open
wide. Bryan decided to look around.*
Yes – all the sentences are the same length,
which makes the writing sound repetitive.

Is this next paragraph any better?

*Bryan walked out of the
school gates and gazed
across the town. It was
raining and the streets were
deserted. The old factory
loomed in front of him and he
stared at it. No one worked
there any more but its doors
were open wide and Bryan
decided to look around.*

This time the writing sounds odd because there are
too many compound sentences.

What about this?
*As Bryan walked out of the school gates, he gazed
across the town. Because it was raining, the streets
were deserted. Looming in front of him was the old*

factory, which he stared at. Although no one worked there any more, its doors were open wide. Deciding to look around, Bryan went in.

The writing still sounds odd, doesn't it? In this case, there are too many complex sentences.

Finally, read this:

As Bryan walked out of the school gates, he gazed across the town. It was raining and the streets were deserted. Where is everybody? he thought. Then he stared. The old factory loomed in front of him. Although no one worked there any more, its doors were open wide. "Now's my chance!" he muttered, deciding to look around.

This time the writing is good because different types of sentence are used.

☆ Simple sentences are useful for drama and clarity, for example: *Then he stared.*

☆ Compound sentences are easy to read. They keep a story flowing smoothly along, for example: *It was raining and the streets were deserted.*

☆ Complex sentences can add extra layers of meaning, for example: *Although no one worked there any more, its doors were open wide.*

Complex sentences help you to suggest, explain, justify, reason, argue, show what is happening elsewhere, or give alternative views.

☆ Questions help to draw your readers into the action: *Where is everybody? he thought.*

☆ Exclamations help to add emphasis and drama: *"Now's my chance!"*

WRITING TIP

You can add extra information to a sentence by dropping in a phrase, clause or simile between commas. For example: The creature rushed towards Sara...

The creature, long-legged and scaly, rushed towards Sara...

The creature, which had been asleep, rushed towards Sara...

The creature, quick as a snake, rushed towards Sara...

PACE YOURSELF

As you write, try to picture the action in your mind. Watch what happens. Remember that you don't need to write down every detail – too much description can slow the pace of a story. So keep your plot going by focusing on the key scenes. Miss out anything that isn't essential. For instance, you don't need to write about every meal your characters eat, or what they do when they're going to bed – unless these scenes develop your plot or tell your readers something new about the characters.

On the other hand, don't rush the story to the point where you simply report what happened. For example, look at this dreadful ending: *The sun came up. The vampire shrivelled into dust. Freda and Fernando went home.*

Try using connectives to miss out boring bits while keeping the pace moving. Flick through some stories and jot down in your writing journal some typical paragraph openers, such as: suddenly, in a flash, at that moment, later that afternoon, in the morning, without warning, after breakfast.

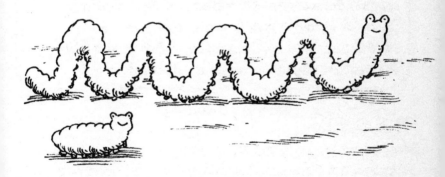

A SHORT STORY OR A LONG YARN?

Before you start writing, think about how long you want your story to be. You don't have to decide on an exact number of words or pages, but it's good to have a general idea of the overall length you're aiming for. For instance, do you want to write a short story?

Or a whole novel,
with chapters and
illustrations? How much
time do you have for your
writing? An hour? A day?
A week or more?

Look at your plan and decide whether each
part of your story will be one paragraph, a couple
of paragraphs or a whole chapter. If you do this,
you can make sure that each section of your story
is evenly balanced.

TIME TO WRITE

You are almost ready to start your story.
First, brainstorm some ideas and jot them
down in your writing journal. Think about:

★ character description, action and dialogue;
★ premonitions;
★ ghosts, ghouls, mutants and monsters;
★ powerful and precise words to use;
★ similes, metaphors and personification;
★ alliteration and onomatopoeia;
★ some exciting exclamations;
★ some useful questions to interest your readers;
★ some powerful sentences.

Use these ideas later on if you get stuck when
you're writing your story.

PUTTING PEN TO PAPER

KICK–START YOUR WRITING

Ready to write? Before you finally start, read
this chapter. Each section will help you through
a different stage of your story.

MAKE A FLYING START
Would you want to read a story that started like this?
Sam went to the shop and bought some turnips. Riveting
stuff, eh? What you need to start your chiller is a sentence
that will really make your readers want to read on. Here
are some ideas.

1 Start with the name of your main character

For example: *Sandy stared
at the government laboratory.*
This introduces the main
character straight away.
It can also help to get the
action going, for example:
*Ali's skin crawled as the
key turned in the lock...*

2 Use a spoken question

For example: *"Have you seen this strange old book before?"* or *"Wherever is that thick smoke coming from?"* This raises a question in the reader's mind and helps to start off the action.

3 Use an exclamation

For example: *"Not so fast!"* or *"I warned you not to touch it!"*. This provides a surprise at the start of the story that will grab the reader's attention.

4 Use or suggest a frightening situation

For example: *She screamed as the hand clutched at her.* Or *She jolted awake. A scream filled the room.* This plunges the reader straight into the story.

5 Use a chilling setting

For example: *Bleak Marsh was a boggy place where damp mists always swirled, even in the summer...*

6 Hint at your ghost, ghoul, mutant or monster

For example: *Werewolves only come out when the moon is full.* Or: *There were three very good reasons for Jamal to believe in ghosts...*

FIRST PARAGRAPHS – ATTENTION-GRABBERS

Try using your opening paragraph to create an eerie, spine-tingling atmosphere. Think about the following:

☆ **Where?**

Where is your main character? What can he see and hear? How does he feel?

☆ **When?**

Choose an unusual time – such as very late at night. Also think about the time of year and the weather.

☆ **Why?**

Why is your main character there? Give an ordinary reason.

☆ **What?**

What happens? Something unusual needs to happen to trigger the story into being frightening. Give a simple clue, such as a sound or something a character sees.

You might want to end your first paragraph on a disturbing note, something that suggests all is not well.

Sim blew on his hands. It was cold at the bus stop. He leant against the peeling bus sign, staring at the leaves shuffling in the darkness of the gutter.

The curved moon cast a silvery light across the street. Sim glanced at his watch. Surely his parents should be here by now? It was then that he saw the lights of the bus in the distance, and watched it rumbling towards the stop. That's strange, he thought, glancing at the timetable. The last bus should have gone ages ago.

THE SECOND PARAGRAPH — PULSE-RAISERS

Now you need to start building tension. One way to do this is to make your main character feel confident and safe in your second paragraph, not noticing that the situation is becoming more and more spooky.

Sim thought of the local ghost story James had told him – the rumour about a ghost bus that snatched people away on a journey to nowhere. A load of old nonsense, he told himself. Sim peered into the distance. It was getting very late and there was still no sign of his parents. Perhaps he should catch the bus after all.

If you have two main characters, you could create tension by sending one away, leaving the other one alone. *Sara and Sean gazed at the swings, quite still in the* darkness. "Look, there's the slide you fell off when we were in Mrs Potter's class," said Sara. They both laughed.

"OK, my mum will kill me if I don't get going," said Sean. "Why don't you come back to my place? I'm sure my dad would drive you home later."

"It's OK, Sean. I'm not a baby. You go. I'll make my own way back."

NAIL-BITERS

You've made your readers want to shout out and warn your main character that she is heading for danger! But your main character is happy, thinking that everything is OK. Now it's time to introduce a nasty surprise that will create suspense and fear. Your character might hear something suspicious, such as footsteps, a twig snapping, or a scratching noise. Or she might see something odd, such as an eye, a hand, or a shadow moving. Maybe she simply senses that something is not quite right, or has a feeling that she is being watched.

When writing a suspense paragraph, there are a number of tactics you can use.

☆ Use short sentences to create dramatic tension and mimic a fast heartbeat.

☆ Balance these with longer sentences which add frightening detail.

☆ Don't reveal what makes the noise or what is seen – keep your monster hidden and your readers guessing.

☆ Make your main character ask a question or think aloud. For example: *"Who's there?" called Sara.* Or: *"Pull yourself together," she muttered under her breath.*

☆ Show how the characters feel by describing their reactions. For instance: *Her hand gripped the park railings until her knuckles turned white.*

To create suspense and fear in the Sara and Sean story, your third paragraph might move straight into making the park darker and more lonely:

Sara began to walk along the path that led to the other side of the park. The trees made the path even darker. The bushes crowded round on all sides. Sara was aware of her own footsteps, clicking in the silence.

You might use noises to build more tension:

Soon Sara reached the iron railings that ran round the south side of the park. She followed them, heading for the exit. A sudden rustle made her turn sharply. "Get a grip!" she muttered, through clenched teeth.

Your character might head for safety:

Sara strode down the path, panting as she went. She needed to be out on the street where the lights were bright, where the cars streamed by, where there were people.

Time for the nasty surprise!
Don't tell your reader everything straight away...
Someone – or something – was blocking the way. Sara stopped, her heart thudding, her throat tight. The figure seemed to be looking right at her.

Now you have a decision to make. Will this nasty surprise turn out to be something ordinary or not?
To her relief, Sara realized that it must be the park attendant. Yes, he wore a cap and a dark suit. He was holding a broom too. He was just rounding up late stragglers!

Sara rushed towards the gate. But as she looked up into the attendant's face she saw – not a face, but a white shape where a face had once been. Sara opened her mouth to scream, but it was too late...

WRITING CLIFFHANGERS

Cliffhangers are events that keep readers on the edge
of their seats by putting the main character into danger.
*I made my way up, one step at a time. The boards
creaked, and in the silence of the empty house the
sound seemed explosive. At the top I paused. A bedroom
door swung open. A dark shadow
shifted. Dust shimmered. A draft
of cold air touched my face.
"Get a grip," I thought. But the
door swung back again, too
quickly. I knew that someone
had to be behind it.*

Many chiller novels use
a cliffhanger at the end of
each chapter, so the reader
is desperate to read on.
This is why people sometimes
say that a book was so exciting they couldn't put it down.
No sooner has the character escaped from one perilous
situation than there is a build-up into another.

48

You could use the following situations as cliffhangers.

✩ The main character senses that someone is behind her.

✩ The main character is locked in a room, or knocked unconscious, or swept into a short struggle with a stranger.

✩ The main character suddenly becomes aware that a stranger is not what they seem. Perhaps the stranger's eyes turn bloodshot. Or the main character glimpses that the stranger's gloved hand is in fact a claw. Or that the stranger has a tongue like a snake...

✩ The main character finds something mysterious or sinister, such as a trail of stinking mud or some bloodstained clothing.

✩ The main 'good' character is about to be captured by a ghost, ghoul, mutant or monster.

✩ The main character is recognized by someone she has never met before.

TYING UP YOUR TALE

Ending your story can be much more difficult than starting it. Here is the worst ending in the world: *Then I woke up and it was all a dream.* This is dead lazy. No reader will thank you for not taking time and care over a decent ending.

Think about some of these ways to end your tale.

1 Return to the start

Take your characters back to the setting where the tale began. Then tie up the problem that has dogged them by defeating the monster – whether it is a vampire on the loose, or a poltergeist, or just a plain ordinary ghost!

2 Take your characters home

Once your ghost, ghoul, mutant or monster has been exterminated, you could tack on a final paragraph in which the main characters make their way home. This helps to lead your readers gently out of the tale and leaves them feeling safe and satisfied.

3 Leave your story on a question

Finishing your story on a question suggests that there might be another story (a sequel) and leaves your readers wondering. For example: *They wondered whether it would be the last time they would hear the high, lonely call of the wolfman.*

4 Show a change in your main character

Look back at the opening of your story and see how your main character was feeling, what sort of person they were. Perhaps they have changed because of what they have been through? Show the change in something your character says or does. For example: *Grinning to herself, Paula marched down the street. She wanted to punch the air and sing.*

You could also show change by using the weather. If you describe the sun breaking through the clouds or the mist clearing, your readers will feel that things are all right now.

5 Leave one loose thread

Ending a chiller by leaving one loose thread is a cunning trick that continues suspense. The main characters think that everything is sorted out and that all is well. But there is one thing they forget about or overlook – one loose end only the reader notices.

Sara and Sean looked at the steaming puddle on the floor.

"Come on, let's get out of here," grinned Sean.

He took Sara's hand and they ran joyfully out into the daylight... leaving the zombie's amulet lying forgotten in the corner of the cave, glowing in the darkness.

6 Reflect on the story

Once the tale has been wrapped up, you could add on an extra paragraph in which there is some thinking about the story, about what has happened and what it means. This can be done in different ways.

☆ The main character thinks aloud. For example:
Frances wondered whether she would ever see Jo again. They had been through so much together. Frances smiled to herself. Yes – they would always be friends.

✿ Two main characters discuss what
    has happened. For example:
    "I'm glad that's over," Simon panted.
    "Me too," breathed Alec.
    *"Let's promise never to go near
the churchyard ever again."*
    And the two boys shook on it.

✿ An adult comments. This can add humour. For instance,
    the two main characters have defeated a terrible
    creature. When they get home, Mum says:
    *"Where on earth have you two been? And those
trainers were new yesterday – they are DISGUSTING!"*

✿ It might be a narrator who comments:
    *And so Ben never did play for Manchester United
    after all. But that is how he came to be the finest
    ghostbuster the world has ever known.*

Now it's time to write your story!

1 Go back to your story planner and double-check the shape of your tale. If you have had any better ideas, now is the time to make some adjustments. Keep your plan by your elbow as you write. You can add new scenes and make changes as you write, but use your plan as your guide to keep your tale on track.

2 While you are writing, you may find that sometimes your story just flows, while on other occasions you may get stuck. Don't worry – this happens to every writer. If you get stuck, you could try:
★ looking at your plan to see what could happen next;
★ taking the character to a new setting;
★ introducing a new character;
★ making something unexpected happen.
If you are still stuck, you might want to:
★ jot down some possible scenes and then choose one;
★ go for a walk and come back to your story later;
★ talk your story through with a friend;
★ re-read your story so far.
If none of these things help, why not leave your story for a few days and see if a new idea pops into your head?

Now – start writing! Good luck!

EDITING AND PUBLISHING

POLISHING YOUR TALE

So you've written your story – well done!
  What next?
  Well, before you can say that your chiller
is finished, you need to check it over. Look for
two things. First, can the writing be improved?
Second, is the writing accurate?

EDITING YOUR STORY

It can help to tuck your story away for a few weeks.
  When you get it out again, you will feel more like
    a reader than the writer. Now, is the story
      frightening? Does it make you want to read
        on? Does it chill the blood? Try reading
        your story aloud – it helps you to hear
        how good it sounds. You may feel a
        bit silly doing this, but it does work!
          Ask a friend to read your story
          through and tell you their favourite
          parts. See if they can find a few

places where they think your story might be improved. All the stories that you buy from bookshops have been checked like this by an editor.

Here are some of the things that you (or your friend) should look for.

1 Possible improvements

☆ Have you used weak words or written clumsy sentences?

☆ Do the sentences in some paragraphs need varying?

☆ Is any dialogue awkward and difficult to follow?

☆ Have you made sure that the characters sound real by showing the sort of person they are and how they feel?

☆ Are some parts of the story too rushed?

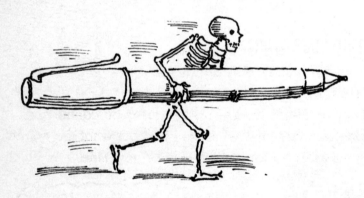

☆ Is there enough suspense?

☆ Have you used cliffhangers?

☆ Do the settings help to create a chilling atmosphere?

☆ Does the story make sense?

2 Checking for accuracy
☆ Make sure that your spelling, punctuation
   and paragraphing are all correct.

Spelling checklist
If you cannot remember a spelling, you can:
☆ Say the word slowly, listen to each sound
   and write them down.
☆ Write the word down, look
   at it and adjust the spelling
   till the word looks right.
☆ Think of a word you can spell
   that rhymes with the word
   you want. The spellings
   might be similar.
☆ Work out if there are any
   suffixes, prefixes or a root
   word that you can spell.
☆ Break the word into syllables
   and tackle each part at a time.
☆ Use a dictionary or spell check.
   Don't avoid using a word because you cannot spell it.
   Do your best, and when you find out what the correct
   spelling is, try to remember it for next time.

Punctuation checklist

☆ Make sure that each sentence makes sense and uses a verb (unless it is a one word sentence, such as: *"OK?"*)

☆ Don't forget exclamation marks after exclamations, such as: *Get out!*

Get out!

☆ Don't forget question marks after questions, such as: *What do you want?*

☆ Don't forget commas to separate the things in a list – apart from before the final 'and'. For example: *Out of the box came boots, scarves, coats, hats and pyjamas!*

☆ Use a comma to separate an adverb start, such as: *Slowly, he turned.*

☆ Use a comma to separate 'ing' and 'ed' starts, such as: *Slipping, she tumbled.*

☆ Use a comma to separate a subordinate clause at the start of a sentence, such as: *Although they were cold, they stayed outside.*

☆ Use a comma when you drop a phrase or clause into a sentence, such as: *Tom, whose hand was bleeding, ran downstairs.*

☆ Use speech marks to surround what is spoken (including any punctuation marks in the speech). Use a comma to lead into what is said. When a new speaker says something, start on a new line. For example:

"Hello," said Kira.
Sam replied, "Hi, how are you?"

Paragraph checklist

Long paragraphs can be hard to read. Don't put off your readers! Start a new paragraph for:

☆ A change of time, for example: *Later that afternoon...*

☆ A change of place, for example: *Back at the police station...*

☆ A change of action, for example: *An explosion ripped through the silence...*

☆ A change of view, for example: *Mrs Savage stared back at Ben and wondered to herself...*

PUBLISHING YOUR STORY

Having spent all this time and effort on writing your story, you now want some readers. You could publish your story in lots of different ways:

☆ read it aloud;
☆ e-mail it to friends;
☆ turn it into a booklet to give to people;
☆ make a tape recording of it;
☆ post it on a website.

USEFUL ADDRESSES

☆ Young Writer

This is the national magazine for young writers – and it's brilliant! It has lots of ideas and tips about writing, in-depth interviews with well-known writers and competitions to enter. It also publishes young writers' stories and poems. You can visit the magazine's website at www.youngwriter.org or phone 01544 318901.

☆ www.stonesoup.com

This website belongs to another magazine for young writers. It provides links to loads of other great sites. These will put you in touch with other young writers, and give you top writing tips and opportunities to publish your writing on the web.

WRITING TIP

Don't forget to give your story an attention-grabbing title. Most writers leave this until the very last thing. (They just use a simple working title while they are writing.) Find the right title – and you're finished! Now, ready for your next chiller?

GLOSSARY

adjective A word that describes somebody or something, eg *the red fish*.

adverb A word that adds meaning to a verb, eg *She ran quickly*.

alliteration A sound effect caused when a letter is repeated in words close together, eg *They ran round the rugged rocks*.

clause A group of words built around a verb, eg *She was thirsty, but she didn't drink*.

cliffhanger An exciting section in a story that ends abruptly, leaving a character in danger.

comma A punctuation mark (,) used to separate parts of a sentence or items in a list.

conjunction A word that links clauses or phrases within sentences, eg *Tom was silent and Jerry knew it was the end!*

connective A word or phrase used to link events in a story, eg *The next morning the robbers woke early*.

dialogue The words that characters speak.

dilemma A problem that characters have to solve.

dramatic tension When the story makes the reader feel anxious.

editing Re-reading a story to improve and correct it.

exclamation A sudden expression of emotion using an exclamation mark, eg *No!*

metaphor The technique of writing about something as if it were something else, eg *Sue scampered away on mouse's paws*.

noun A word that names something or somebody, eg *The lorry stopped by the shop*.

onomatopoeia Words which sound like their meaning, eg hiss, cuckoo, buzz, crack.

paragraph A group of sentences that make up a section of writing. New paragraphs begin at a change of time, place, speaker or focus.

personification A technique in which objects are given human characteristics, eg *The wind moaned.*

phrase A group of words that work as one unit, eg *the grey-haired, old lady.*

prepositional phrase A phrase that begins with a preposition, eg *over the road, down the lane, across the street.*

simile A technique in which the writer compares one thing to another, eg *The moon was like a thin smile* or *The moon was thin as a fingernail.*

speech verb A verb used to state how dialogue is spoken, eg *said* or *hissed, muttered, complained*, etc.

stylistic devices Writing techniques that add impact to writing, eg alliteration, onomatopoeia, simile, metaphor and personification.

thesaurus A type of dictionary that provides alternatives to words, eg *eat – scoff, chew, munch, gobble*, etc.

trigger An event that starts the action moving in a story.

verb A 'being' or 'doing' word, eg *She <u>crawled</u> down the lane. She <u>felt</u> petrified.*

INDEX